Hydroponic

Discover How to Build a Simple Hydroponic Technology at Home in Less Than 24hr

By Gardenfluencer Tech

© Copyright 2018 - All rights reserved.

The content contained within this book may not be reproduced, duplicated or transmitted without direct written permission from the author or the publisher.

Under no circumstances will any blame or legal responsibility be held against the publisher, or author, for any damages, reparation, or monetary loss due to the information contained within this book. Either directly or indirectly.

Legal Notice:

This book is copyright protected. This book is only for personal use. You cannot amend, distribute, sell, use, quote or paraphrase any part, or the content within this book, without the consent of the author or publisher.

Disclaimer Notice:

Please note the information contained within this document is for educational and entertainment purposes only. All effort has been executed to present accurate, up to date, and reliable, complete information. No warranties of any kind are declared or implied. Readers acknowledge that the author is not engaging in the rendering of legal, financial, medical or professional advice. The content within this book has been derived from various sources. Please consult a licensed professional before attempting any techniques outlined in this book.

By reading this document, the reader agrees

that under no circumstances is the author responsible for any losses, direct or indirect, which are incurred as a result of the use of information contained within this document, including, but not limited to, — errors, omissions, or inaccuracies.

Free Bonus!

A Cheat Sheet of 10 Unrestricted Indoor Gardening Tips for Beginners to Start Growing Immediately (Additional pH & Nutrient Table for Hydroponic Plants)

https://bit.ly/2T18mI6

Simply as a 'Thank You' for purchasing this book, take this **FREE PDF Cheat Sheet and Additional pH & Nutrient Table for**

Hydroponic Plants by accessing on the link above to help you get started off on your hydroponic journey. These are some tips of indoor gardening that will **definitely give you a head start** on building your hydroponic system. It includes tip with dealing indoor plants insects, caring your plants, choosing the right indoor plant and many more. Furthermore, there is a simple instruction on building a DIY Craft for gardening that even you can do it together with your children's.

Table Of Contents

Table of Contents

Introduction 12
Chapter One: Types of Hydroponic Systems 19

Type 1: Wick System (Difficulty level- Beginner [1/5]) 21
Pros 23
Cons 23

Type 2: Deep Water Culture (DWC) System (Difficulty level- Beginner [2/5]) 24
Pros 25
Cons 26

Type 3: Nutrient Film Technique (NFT) (Difficulty level- Advanced [4/5]) 27
Pros 28
Cons 29

Type 4: Ebb and Flow System (Difficulty level- Intermediate [3/5]) 30
Pros 32
Cons 32

Type 5: Aeroponics System (Difficulty level- Advanced [4.5/5]) 33
Pros 35

Cons 35

Type 6: Drip Systems (Difficulty level- Intermediate [3/5]) 36
Pros 37
Cons 37

Chapter Two: Building a Hydroponic System *39*

Hydroponics Wick System 39
Step 1: The problem 39
Step 2: What you will need 40
Step 3: Place the brick in the pot............................41
Step 4: Prep the pot for the wick 41
Step 5: Prepare the wick 42
Step 6: Prep the soil and fill up the pot 42
Step 7: Add the plant..43
Step 8: Add the watertight container 44

DWC System 45
Step 1: Gather the materials...................................45
Step 2: Air tubing holes 47
Step 3: Mesh potholes...48
Step 4: Connect the air system 49
Step 5: Done!..49

NFT (Nutrient Film Technique) System .50
Step 1: Gather materials 51
Step 2: Build the channel 52
Step 3: Build the reservoir 53
Step 4: Assembling it all...54
Step 5: Maintenance...56

Ebb and Flow System............................57

Materials and supplies 58
Keep in mind 60
Basic steps 61

Types of setups 63
Plant containers in series 63
Flooding tray design 64
Aeroponics 65

Drip Irrigation 70
Step 1: Gather supplies 71
Step 2: Cut a hole 72
Step 3: Nutrient mixture 73
Step 4: Adjustments 74
Step 5: Done 74

Chapter Three: Hydroponic Seed Starting 77

Benefits of Starting with Seeds 77

Things Needed to Start Seeds 79

Steps for Sprouting Seeds 80

Steps for Transplantation 82

Chapter Four: Best Plants for Hydroponics 84

Lettuces 85

Tomatoes 86

Radishes 87

Kale 89

Cucumbers 90
Spinach 92
Beans 93
Chives 94
Basil 95
Mint 96
Strawberries 98
Blueberries 99
Peppers 100

Chapter Five: Hydroponic Nutrients.103
Selecting the Nutrients 104
Nutrient Mixture 108

Chapter Six: Lighting Guide 111

Chapter Seven: Maintenance and Troubleshooting 114
Keep it Clean 114
Drippers 115
Ebb and Flow System 115
pH 116
Calcium Deficiency 117
Incorrect Lighting 117

Nutrient Deficiency 118

Algae Growth 119

Pests and Pathogens 120

Conclusion 123

Bonus Materials 126

Introduction

Well, what if I told you that you don't need soil to grow plants? Yes, you read it right, you no longer need soil to grow plants. That sounds extraordinary, doesn't it? Well, it's true. Instead, you submerge their roots in water to grow them—growing plants without using soil is known as hydroponics (which is a combination of two Greek words that mean water and toil). It might sound funny, but a lot of the food that we consume these days is produced hydroponically.

The process through which plants grow is called photosynthesis. In photosynthesis, plants use sunlight along with the chlorophyll present in their leaves to turn carbon dioxide and water into oxygen and glucose. The chemical equation for photosynthesis is:

$$6CO_2 + 6H_2O \rightarrow C_6H_{12}O_6 + 6O_2$$

Do you notice any mention of soil in this equation? You don't, do you? That's because soil is not necessary for the growth of a plant. They can photosynthesize without any soil, and a soilless medium like coconut coir or expandable clay pellets will suffice. So, if plants can obtain their requirements from another source—say, by dipping their roots into a nutrient-enriched mixture of water—then soil can, altogether, be eliminated from the picture. This is the principle upon which hydroponics is based.

So, what are the benefits of hydroponics and why should one opt for this over conventional gardening options?

Hydroponics encourages space saving when compared to conventional methods of soil gardening. Usually, a plant's roots need lots of space to spread under the soil. Well, not anymore. You merely need to submerge the roots in an oxygenated, nutrient-rich solution. Imagine if it were possible for you to obtain all the nutrition that your body needs by popping a single pill—you no longer have to consume three meals a day. Instead of using soil as the medium to carry nutrients, a customized nutrient mixture continues to provide nutrition to the plant, continuously. This comes in handy because it enables you to grow plants packed together. Space saving is a great advantage, especially these days when space is becoming more scarce.

Hydroponics also helps you save water, which sounds a bit strange when you think of water being essential for this process. But before you decide to jump to any conclusions, how often do you think a gardener needs to water their plants? Usually, it's every alternate day so that the soil soaks up the water and is transported to the roots. That sounds fine, doesn't it? But that's only a portion of the big picture. Some of the water is bound to seep out of the container, some of it evaporates, and a portion of it seeps further into the soil beyond the plant's roots. So, in practice, the plant essentially only uses up a small portion of the water. Hydroponics uses a simple recirculating mechanism that ensures that the water is fully soaked up by the roots. It means that the portion of water that isn't absorbed by the plant is directly sent to the reservoir. The same water from the reservoir is later pumped up to the plants. Since the reservoir is shut tight, there is no chance for the water to evaporate, and it certainly will not seep out of the bottom of the container. You can save around 80% of the water by switching to hydroponics instead of using regular soil gardening.

One of the common reasons why a lot of people don't opt for gardening is because they are worried about weeding. There is an easy way out of this—hydroponics. If there is no soil, then there are no weeds, which is rather simple and obvious. Also, the lack of soil pretty much eliminates all pests and disease—when you take out soil from the picture and replace it with a soilless medium, it removes the chances of the plant attracting any soil-borne pests and diseases that are rampant in conventional gardening.

Hydroponics also saves you time since you don't have to worry about pests, weeding and watering. Apart from this, it also speeds up the growth of a plant. So, it essentially creates a double-headed time-saving option.

Apart from the benefits above, hydroponics gives you complete control over the growth of the plants. You can select the way you want to grow the plants when to grow them, and even the nutrient mixture to feed them. If the idea of organically grown produce appeals to you, then this is the best method of gardening. Not only is it cheaper to grow your produce, but you can also use this to spruce up your house—if you want to grow indoor plants without any hassle, then opt for hydroponics.

I want to thank you for choosing this book. This book aims to provide you with information that will help you pick a method of hydroponics that works extremely well for you. You will learn about the different methods of hydroponics, how to build your hydroponic garden at home, the types of nutrients you can use, how to plant your hydroponic garden, how to create nutrient mixes, and the solutions to certain common problems to protect your plants. If you are ready to learn more about hydroponics and how you can set up a hydroponic garden at home, then let us start without further ado!

Chapter One: Types of Hydroponic Systems

The art of hydroponics has certainly been around for centuries and it is believed to be as old as the pyramids. The Hanging Garden of Babylon, one of the Seven Wonders of the world uses a rudimentary form of hydroponics. Hydroponics have been used since ages to grow rice. In 1934, a professor at the University of California started to use this technique to grow other crops. The result was that he managed to grow tomato vines that were 25-feet long and had to be harvested using ladders.

This is how modern hydroponics has come into being and it's been developing ever since. During the Second World War, this technique was used to grow vegetables, for feeding the Allied soldiers- on the air force and naval bases in the South Pacific region. Today, hydroponic systems are used to feed millions of people living in the arid regions of Israel, Lebanon, Kuwait as well as the islands of Ceylon, Philippines and Canaries. Did you know that more than half of the tomatoes harvested in Vancouver Island and one fifth of the tomato crop in Moscow are produced using hydroponics? There are well developed hydroponic systems aboard the American nuclear submarines and Russian space stations as well. Even the remotest regions on this earth make use of this technique for domestic purposes.

In this section, you will learn about the six different types of hydroponic systems that you can choose from, along with their advantages and disadvantages.

Type 1: Wick System (Difficulty level- Beginner [1/5])

Wick

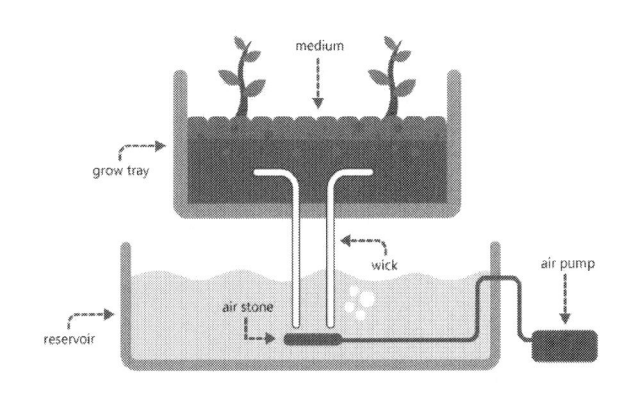

Involves no moving parts, can use variety of growing media. Nutrient solution is realesed onto growing tray and delivered to the roots through the wick.

A wick hydroponic system is the simplest of all

the hydroponic systems you can build. The concept of this system has been around for ages, but it wasn't thought of as a hydroponic system in the past. This is considered to be a system of passive hydroponics—you don't need any air or water pumps for it. Nutrients, as well as water, are transported to the plant's roots through a wick, which can be a piece of felt or rope. The success of a wicking system primarily depends on the growing medium that you use, with the ideal choices being coconut coir, vermiculture, or even perlite.

Wick systems are ideal for small plants that don't need a lot of water or nutrients. This doesn't mean that you cannot grow large plants, but the nutritional and water needs of a larger plant cannot be easily sustained with this system.

Pros

- If you manage to set it up properly, then the hydroponics system will be truly "hands-free."

- It is a great option for growing small plants, especially for gardeners who are just getting started.

Cons

- It's not ideal for larger plants.

- If the wicks aren't placed correctly or if you don't use the right medium, then it can kill your plants.

Type 2: Deep Water Culture (DWC) System (Difficulty level- Beginner [2/5])

Water Culture Or **Aquaponic**

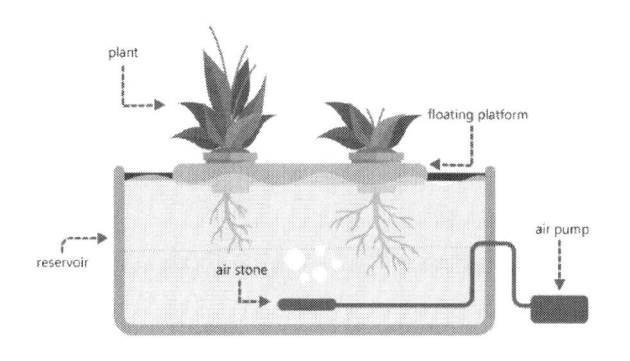

Containers hold plants inside floating Styrofoam platform - roots suspended directly into the nutrient water.

A deep water culture system—or DWC—is a

simple hydroponic system. In this system, you will need a reservoir to accommodate the nutrient solution. The roots of the plants are suspended in this solution so that they have a constant supply of all the things that they need for their growth—oxygen, water, and nutrients.

An air stone or an air pump is used to oxygenate the nutrient solution. This prevents the plant from drowning in water. The plants will be placed in net pots resting on a foam board or on the top of a container (the one that you are using as a reservoir). Add some hydroponic growing medium to the pots, and that's about it.

Pros

- It's the least expensive method of hydroponics and is easily created.

- It's low-maintenance.
- Recirculation of the nutrient solution, therefore, less wastage.

Cons

- You cannot grow large plants.
- If the plant has a rather long growing period, then this isn't suitable.

Type 3: Nutrient Film Technique (NFT) (Difficulty level- Advanced [4/5])

Nutrient Film Technique (NFT)

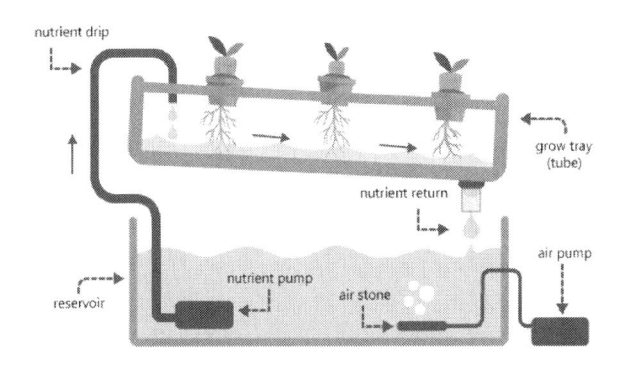

A continuous flow of nutrients eliminates need for timer. Pump forces nutrient solution over plant roots onto "grow tray," then overflow drains into reservoir.

This is a popular form of a commercial system of hydroponics. In this method, the plants are all grown in channels that have a nutrient solution constantly pumping through them, which runs along the bottom of the channel. When this solution reaches the end of the channel, it goes back into the main reservoir and is sent to the starting point, and the cycle restarts. Just like the DWC system, this is also a means of recirculation. In a DWC system, the roots are submerged in the nutrient solution, but in NFT they aren't. Instead, the plants are placed in the channel in net pots along with a growing medium.

Pros

- NFT doesn't need a lot of growing medium.

- It's a system of recirculation, so there isn't much wastage.

Cons

- Any pump failure can essentially kill your plants.

- If the roots start to overgrow, then they will clog up the channels.

Type 4: Ebb and Flow System (Difficulty level- Intermediate [3/5])

Ebb and Flow Or **Flood and Drain**

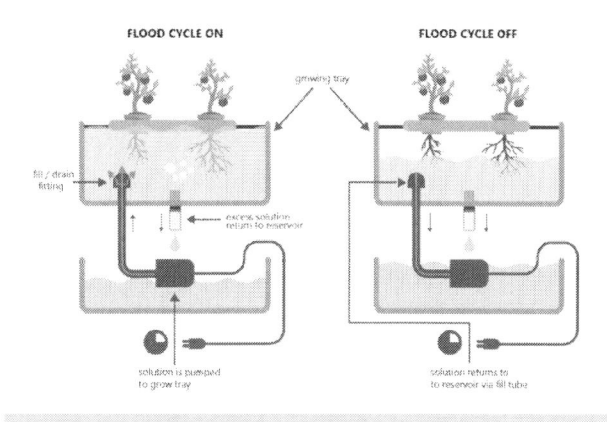

Utilizes submerged pump connected to timer to control temporarily flooding root zone's grow to tray with nutrient solution which drains back to reservoir.

The ebb and flow system is also known as the flood and drain system. Unlike the previous systems, this one doesn't expose the roots of your plants to the nutrient solution. Instead, you will need to grow the plants in a tray that's lined with growing medium. This tray will then be flooded with the nutrient solution a couple of times per day. The number of times the tray needs to be flooded depends on a couple of factors, like the size of the plants, their water requirement, air temperature, their stage of growth, and so on.

A reservoir with the nutrient solution is placed under the tray, and the water is pumped into the tray with a water pump—a timer is essential to schedule the flooding. Once the tray is flooded, then gravity will do its work, and the solution is drawn back into the reservoir. After this, the nutrient solution is re-oxygenated, and then it merely needs to wait for the next cycle.

Pros

- It offers a great deal of flexibility regarding the growing medium used and the organization of the plants.

- It's quite efficient with regards to the water and energy that's used.

Cons

- If the environmental conditions aren't favorable, or if you don't control them properly, then the roots will dry out quickly.

- You need to use a lot of growing medium. So, if you don't opt for the right growing media, then you will essentially be killing the plants.

Type 5: Aeroponics System (Difficulty level- Advanced [4.5/5])

Aeroponic

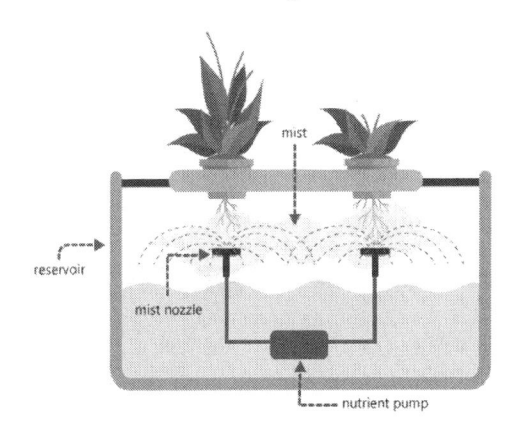

Also known as "fogponics," plant roots not suspended in water but hang in the air receiving nutrients-rich growing medium via misting.

This is one of the most sophisticated and high-tech hydroponics systems that you can use. Once you understand how it works, it is easy to use.

An aeroponic system is quite similar to an NFT system—suspension of the roots in the air. The primary difference is that, in this system, it uses misting to constantly supply the roots with the nutrient solution instead of using a film of nutrient solution.

Some people tend to opt to mist their plants on a cycle, like in the ebb and flow system, but the cycles here are not as lengthy, and the waiting time between each misting is only a couple of minutes. If you are using a finer sprayer, then you can also mist the plants continuously, to ensure that the roots are getting all the oxygen that they need.

Pros

- It's quicker to grow plants using this system when compared to a deep-water culture system.

- The roots can obtain more oxygen when compared to other forms of hydroponics in which the roots are submerged.

Cons

- If the high-pressure nozzles fail, then the roots will dry out.

- It's more complicated to set up than the other methods and is slightly expensive.

Type 6: Drip Systems (Difficulty level- Intermediate [3/5])

Drip
recovery or non-recovery

Recirculating drip systems recycle excess nutrient solution from reservoir. Timer controls submersed pump to drip nutrient solution onto base of each plant via drip line.

This method of hydroponics is usually used in commercial operations and is seldom used in recreational gardening. The main reason for this is because it is easier to operate it on a large scale and seems like overkill for a small garden. Regardless, it's one of the best methods of hydroponics that you can use.

Pros

- It allows you to have absolute control over the watering and the feeding schedule of the plants.
- It's quite sturdy and is almost fail-proof.
- It's cheaper than the aeroponics system.

Cons

- It's overkill for a small garden.
- pH and nutrient levels will keep fluctuating.

- It'll likely lead to a lot of wastage.

Regardless of the method of hydroponics that you opt for, you will be able to grow plants successfully! Hydroponics offers a great deal of flexibility, so even if you run into any trouble, you will be able to fix it rather easily.

Chapter Two: Building a Hydroponic System

Now that you know about the different hydroponic systems, the next step is to learn to build each of these systems. In this section, you will learn about the simple ways in which you can build each of these systems for less than $100.

Hydroponics Wick System

Step 1: The problem

With a lot of houseplants, the common problem is that they usually have damaged leaf tips, which is due to a poor watering technique. Growers usually let the plants dry out completely, and they overwater them—the idea is to keep the plants' roots moist without overwhelming them.

Step 2: What you will need

You will need:

- a plant that you want to transplant
- a clean towel or rag
- a pot with some drainage holes
- a container that's bigger than the pot and is watertight
- a brick or something that you can use to elevate the pot
- a knife
- soilless growing media like coconut coir

- some slow release fertilizer

Step 3: Place the brick in the pot

If you have a brick, then smash it up and place the pieces inside the watertight container. If you don't have any bricks handy, then try to find something similar.

Step 4: Prep the pot for the wick

If you have a pot with drainage holes at the bottom, then your work is easy. If the pot doesn't have drainage holes, then you need to drill some holes along the circumference of the bottom of the pot. Now, take a knife or a sharp blade and cut a small, circular hole at the center of the bottom of the pot. While cutting out a hole, don't cut toward yourself, to avoid any injuries.

Step 5: Prepare the wick

Take the old towel or rag and cut a strip from it. The length of the strip needs to be equivalent to the height of the pot with drainage in it, and it must be at least a couple of inches wide. Now, you need to roll it up and stick it through the hole you made in the previous step. Once you insert it, keep tugging on it until it is hanging out the bottom of the pot (by at least a couple of inches). The wick needs to be hanging out the bottom and must be able to reach into the bricks while being in the pot.

Step 6: Prep the soil and fill up the pot

Check if the soilless media that you are using has any fertilizer in it. If it doesn't, then you need to add some granules of slow-release fertilizer into it, and then start filling up the pot with the mix. Hold on to the wick while you are filling it up. You need to put sufficient media into the pot such that the top of the media in which your plant is growing right now will lie about an inch below the neck of the pot into which you will transplant it.

Step 7: Add the plant

You will need to remove the plant from its original pot or container. Please check the roots—if you notice that they are tightly wound around the outside of the growing media, then gently dust off the excess. Now place this plant into the pot you prepped and align the wick such that it is directly near the roots of the plant. If the wick seems to be longer than the top of the plant's growing media, then snip away the excess. Now fill up the pot with the soilless media.

Step 8: Add the watertight container

You will need to fill the watertight container with water so that 80% of the brick is submerged. Never fill up water to a level higher than the bricks. It is essential that the drainage holes in the pot can still drain water. Now take the pot holding your plant and place it into the watertight container, in such a manner that the wick reaches the bottom of the watertight container and is submerged in the water. At this point, you will need to water the soilless media if it seems too dry. It is best if the media stays a little moist.

You will end up with a pot holding your pot that's placed in a watertight container containing water. Water will be transported to the roots through the wick. The water level in the pot must never be higher than the bricks placed in it. You will need to water the plant form the top every couple of months so that the excess salts are washed away. As long as there is water in the container, your plant will continue to water itself. So, all in all, you will be able to build a hydroponics watering system within a budget of $50 since all the items you need are easily available and cheap.

DWC System

To build a DWC system at home, it will not cost you more than $20-$35. This system is easy to set up and is cost-effective.

Step 1: Gather the materials

You will need:

- a hand drill (something smaller in

diameter than the plastic tubing you will use)

- a permanent marker or sharpie

- a sharp knife, like a Stanley knife

- small mesh pots (if it is a small container then don't use more than 5 net pots, but it depends on the number of plants you want to grow)

- clay pellets or any other growing media of your choice—a mix of coconut coir and clay pellets

- dual output hydroponics or aquarium pump

- two airstones

- plastic tubing (5 feet long)

- An opaque plastic box (it must not let any light through to avoid the growth of algae or root rot). If you want to increase the size of the plastic box, then you will need to increase the size of the airstones and the number of pots you want to place in it.

Step 2: Air tubing holes

Now you will need to cut holes for air tubing. To do this, you will need to measure the center of the box on one side and mark the spot with the marker. Then, measure 1cm on either side of the center and mark these spots, too. You will need to cut or drill the holes here. Drill the holes and get rid of the burrs with a knife. Once the holes are ready, you will need to insert the air tube through it—it must be a snug fit. Resize the holes accordingly to accommodate the tubing snugly. If the holes are too big, then use some silicone sealant to seal them.

Step 3: Mesh potholes

In this step, you will need to cut holes for placing the net or the mesh pots. The best way to go about this is to place the pots on the lid (according to the placement you want to grow the plants in) and then draw around the pot with a marker. Once you do this, you will need to drill holes inside the ring you carefully drew. Drill within the circle, or else the hole will be too big for the pot, and it will fall through. Use the knife and cut the holes out but be careful not to crack the box. If your box does crack, use some duct tape to fix it. Once you cut out the holes, you need to place the mesh pots in them—check if they fit well or make the changes as needed.

Step 4: Connect the air system

Revisiting the holes that you drilled in step 2, you now need to pass the air tubes through these holes. Connect the tubes to the airstones and the air pump. Place the airstones right below where the plants will be present to ensure that their roots are always oxygenated.

Step 5: Done!

Place the lid on the container along with the pots, and the construction is complete. Before you place the plants into the net pots, you need to line them up with the growing media. You will be left with a big, plastic box that has plants sprouting out of the lid! It's quite simple, isn't it?

NFT (Nutrient Film Technique) System

In this section, you will learn about building your NFT system that will carry a mix of water and nutrients from a reservoir, through a channel (providing nutrients to the plants), and then sending them back into the reservoir. It essentially uses a system of recycling, and the water wastage is virtually non-existent. This system is pretty much hands-free until it is harvest time—so you don't have to worry about the things that you would be fussing over in regular soil gardening, like weeding, watering, or pest control.

Step 1: Gather materials

You will need:

- a 4" wide PVC pipe
- a grow light
- Two pieces of 2x4s
- a storage bin
- 3-inch plastic mesh or net pots
- 6 feet of 3/4" wide vinyl tubing (two pieces—one 10' and another 4'6")
- a submersible pump (preferably of 160 GPH)
- hydroponic nutrient solution, such as Ionic Grow
- growing medium (Growool, clay pellets, perlite or such)

- 2 x 5 inches of PVC flat caps

- Apart from the above, you will need supplies like a drill with a ¾" drill bit, a 3" drill bit and a 1" drill bit, along with some safety gloves.

Step 2: Build the channel

To build the channel for the NFT hydroponics system, you need to cut down a 1'8" channel (the PVC pipe's size needs to be a good fit for the storage bin that you acquire). You will need to drill 3" holes into the top of it and ensure that they are evenly spaced out. These holes will hold the mesh pots in the channel. On the opposite side of the large holes, you will need to drill a 3/8" hole, which will be used to drain the water from the channel.

You will need to drill a 3/8" hole in the middle

of one PVC cap—you will be using this hole for inserting the tube that will carry the water from the reservoir into the channel. Finally, you will need to cut two pieces of wood into an inverted isosceles trapezoid near the top portion of the wood—this wood will ensure that the channel stays stable and doesn't move. You will need another piece of wood to provide the necessary slope to ensure that the channel has a slight slope for the water to flow freely. To determine the slope, you will need to use a 1:30 ratio—for every 30" of its horizontal length, there needs to be a slope of 1".

Step 3: Build the reservoir

Calling the storage bin a reservoir does sound fancy, doesn't it? For getting started, you must drill a 3/8" hole at the far end of the reservoir. This hole will be connected to the holes at the opposite end of the reservoir with 10" black, vinyl tubing.

Once you do this, you will need to drill a 1" hole on the opposite side of the hole you just drilled, but drill this hole towards its right side. This will be the hole to insert the power plug of the submersible pump (it must be about 4-5" above the 1" hole you just drilled). You will be using this for inserting the vinyl tube to pump water into the channel.

Step 4: Assembling it all

You will need to start by inserting the 4'6" tube into the hole that you have drilled closest to the outlet. Then, you will need to insert the 10" tube into the hole at the far end. The next step is to place the submersible pump into the reservoir and then connect it to the longer piece of tube so that it's stable at the bottom of the reservoir. Run the outlet in a 1" hole and then plug it all in, once ready. The next step is to place the indented wood near the far end of the side of the bin with only one hole, and then place the other piece opposite this piece of wood (it essentially needs to create a downward slope into the drainage hole). After this, you can add the PVC channel. You will need to connect the 10" tube to the hole at the bottom of the PVC and then place the longer tube into the PVC cap that you drilled a hole in. You must ensure that the length of the tube within the channel is the same as the length of the tube at the bottom of the pots when they rest in the holes you drilled (to ensure that the water level is such that the roots don't drown).

After all this, you can start adding the nutrient water mixture into the reservoir and power it up. Carefully go through the instructions on the nutrient mix bag to ensure that you don't add too little or too much of it to the water. Ensuring that you mix it thoroughly, you can now turn the pump on. Add the sprouts—or seeds—to the net or mesh pots in which you have filled the growing medium. You then need to place the grow light above the plants, ensuring that they're placed in such a way that they enable photosynthesis without burning the plants.

Step 5: Maintenance

If you have set this up outside, then you need to ensure that the reservoir bin is opaque and doesn't let any light through. If any light enters the bin, then it promotes the growth of algae, and it also deactivates certain nutrients in the mixture. You will need to replenish the nutrient mix every ten days or so. If you want to boost the growth, then you can add natural growth hormones to the crown of the plants—gibberellic acid, for example.

Ebb and Flow System

It is quite easy to build, and you can use materials that are lying around your house to do so, customizing it according to your space availability. Also, you don't have to spend much money on growing and tending to your plants.

The main aspect of this system is one that houses the containers within which you will grow the plants, growing one or multiple plants in containers placed in a series. A timer will control the pump, and this will pump the water-nutrient mix from the reservoir through the tubing into the main part of the system (a submersible pump does this). The nutrient solution will flood the system until it reaches the preset overflow level of the tube so that the roots soak up their dose of nutrients. You will need to place the overflow tube such that it rests 2" below the growing medium you use.

Once the water reaches the overflow limit, the water will start draining back into the reservoir and will be recirculated again. The overflow tube sets the water level in the ebb and flow system while making sure that the water mix doesn't spill out when the pump is on. Once the pump is turned off, the drainage system will siphon the water into the reservoir through the tube.

Materials and supplies

You will need:

- a container to grow the plants in

- a reservoir to house the nutrient mixture

- a submersible pump

- a timer (for turning the pump on and off)

- tubing to run from the pump in the reservoir into the system that needs to be flooded

- an overflow tube with a preset flooding level

- growing medium

There are different ways in which you can build this form of the hydroponic system, and they are ideal for growing small to medium-sized plants—you will need to increase the size of this setup if you want to accommodate larger plants.

You can use anything from a bucket, water

bottles, storage totes, trashcans, and such to fashion this hydroponic system. Once you manage to understand how this system works, you can pretty much use any container to fit this system.

Keep in mind

There are two tips that you need to keep in mind while building an ebb and flow system. The first is that you need to ensure that the air can get to the top of the overflow tube without spilling any water. You can use a "T" connector for this purpose. It ensures that air pockets don't form and also enables smooth flooding and drainage of water.

The second tip is to ensure that the overflow tube is slightly bigger than the tube for the water inlet from the submersible pump. The water will only move through due to gravity, and the water is flowing in through pressure that's building up from the pump. If you don't take care of it, you will end up pumping more water than the system can siphon, and it will result in an overflow.

Basic steps

The first step is to find the right container to house the plants. You might think that a transparent container looks presentable, but it does more harm than good to your plants. The roots, as well as the nutrient solutions, don't react favorably to light so opt for an opaque container.

You will need two boxes to build this system. One box will house the plants, and the other will be the reservoir. It's ideal if the boxes you opt for are such that the growing container sits nicely on the reservoir. If that's not the case, then you can always use a table or something else to sit the growing container nicely on the reservoir.

You will need to drill two holes into the bottom of the container—one is for the inlet, and the other one is for the overflow. The overflow outlet needs to be slightly larger than the inlet one. If you have drilled bigger holes, then you simply need to get bigger tubes. Now you will need to cut a piece out for inserting the hose for the pump and the inlet (the hose must extend from the pump and outlet, and then you need to attach it to the inlet).

Place the growing container on the reservoir to see if it's a good fit. If you feel that the hose is too long, then snip a piece off it. Line the container with the growing media and fill up the reservoir to halfway with plain water.

Now it's time to flood the setup—the maiden flood! Check how long it takes for the water to flood the upper tray. Before you turn on the pump, take a stopwatch to time it. Start the pump and the stopwatch. Once the tray is flooded, stop the pump and stop the stopwatch. This is the time that's necessary to flood the upper tray. Adjust the pump run according to the available natural light. If you know that the light will hit the plants at around 8 am, then flood the container at that time. You will need to flood the container a couple of times daily, so set up the timer according to what you think is the right time for your plants.

Types of setups

Plant containers in series

This is perhaps the most commonly used method of ebb and flow hydroponics. In this design, multiple containers are placed in a series, and all these containers will be flooded simultaneously. It is important to note that the containers housing the plants that need to flood must be placed above the reservoir. The water will be siphoned into the reservoir when gravity does its work, and the draining mechanism will work efficiently.

All the containers will be connected via tubing so that whenever the system is flooded, the plants will receive water immediately. Instead of having a separate overflow limit for each container, there will be a single overflow tube, which will be connected to all the containers at the base. And, whenever the water level reaches the top of this tube, it will simply overflow and revert to the reservoir.

The height of the water level will be based on the height of the overflow tube. By adjusting the height of this single tube, you can tweak the overflow level for all containers.

Flooding tray design

This is a temporary hydroponics system idea, especially when you need to move plants around. Instead of using multiple containers with plants placed in them, you will merely need to use a single container—a shallow one that sits well on the reservoir. The water will be pumped into the tray from the reservoir through one side and will be siphoned in the reservoir from the other side. This ensures that the water is being circulated from one side of the tray to the other. This method usually leaves the tray exposed to the elements and can lead to the growth of algae if you aren't careful.

Aeroponics

You can purchase a hydroponic solution from any of the local hydroponic supply stores, and all that you need to do is follow the directions printed on the label—it's pretty simple. You will need to drain the water out every couple of weeks and replenish the nutrient mixture.

Opting for cloning with aeroponics is a much better method than the regular soil root cuttings. When you are cloning from cuttings, you don't need to add any extra nutrients to the water. As long as the water stays clean, you don't even have to flush the system, and so is a more sterile option when compared to soil cuttings. You need to add tap water, let it run for an hour to get rid of the chlorine, and that's about it.

The most common aeroponics system uses plastic storage bins along with PVC pipe. The size and length of these things will depend on your needs.

Take a large storage bin (50-quart) and turn it upside down. Carefully measure and then drill a hole on either side of the container, about two-thirds from the bottom of it. Ensure that you opt for a container that has a tightly sealed lid that's opaque. The holes must be smaller than the size of the PVC pipe you decide to push through it. For instance, if you opt for three-quarters of an inch PVC pipe, then the hole needs to be seven-eighths of an inch wide. You must ensure that it is at a level and add a couple of inches to the overall length of the PVC pipe (it will come in handy later on). For instance, you must opt for a 32" pipe instead of a 30" pipe. The pipe needs to be long enough so that even when you fit it into the container through the holes on either side, a portion of it will be still sticking out from either side. Now, cut the pipe in half and attach a cap to either side of the pipe. Add three or four small sprayer holes in each section of the pipe. If the pipe is three-quarters of an inch, then the holes need to be one-eighth of an inch each.

Start fitting taps into each of the sprayer holes and clean up any debris that comes along your way. Take each section of the pipe and slide them through the holes in the storage bin. Ensure that the sprayer holes are facing upward. Screw in the sprayers, and we can move on to the next step.

Now, take the extra 2" portions of the PVC pipe and glue them to the bottom of a "T" fitting or connector, which in turn will be connected to the initial two portions of the pipe. Add the adapter to the other end of the smaller pipe, and this will be connected to the hose. The hose must at least be a foot in length. Turn the container such that its right side is facing upward and place the submersible pump within. Place the hose such that one end is clamped to the pump while the other one is clamped on to the adapter. If you want to, you can also add an aquarium heater to the setup (if the plants need it).

Add about eight holes measuring 1½" each to the top of the storage container. Once again, this will depend on the size of the netted pots you are using—select the net pots according to the size you wish. The pots will need to be spaced couple of inches apart. You can use 3.5" to 4" mesh pots for tomatoes and smaller ones for smaller plants like herbs.

You will need to cut holes into the lid of the

container for placing the pots. Use a sharp knife and a drill to do this. The holes that you cut out must be a snug fit for the pots, and the holes must not be too large or else the pots will fall through. Use weather-seal to tape the outside rim.

Now it is time to fill up the container with the nutrient mixture just below the sprayers. Secure the lid and start inserting the growing pots into the lid.

Well, that's about it! You have successfully made an aeroponics system to grow plants!

Drip Irrigation

This method is not only popular with the professionals, but with gardening enthusiasts as well. It is ideal for all sizes of gardens, from commercial farming to growing a single plant. In the version of drip irrigation that's explained in this section, you will be using a 5-gallon bucket that's fixed with a submersible pump at its bottom that helps transport the nutrient solution along the irrigation channel. Spaghetti tubing that is ¼" wide will be connected to the main line, and an emitter—or a dripper—will be connected to the spaghetti tubing.

Most of these supplies are usually provided in a drip irrigation kit. The remaining mixture of nutrients and water will seep out of the bottom of the pot and will revert into the bucket. The feeding frequency will depend on the water retention of the growing medium and the needs of the plants. The feeding frequency can be anywhere between 15 minutes to 3-4 hours.

Here are the steps that you need to follow:

Step 1: Gather supplies

You will need:

- a 5-gallon bucket with a lid
- a 6-inch pot for growing
- a utility knife and a drill for making holes
- a submersible pump with barbed fittings (160 GPH)
- a polytube that fits the pump with a clamp or a plug (tube needs to be three feet long)
- spaghetti tubing
- growing medium
- a drip emitter
- a dripper

The version of drip irrigation system explained in this section helps supply a steady and low-volume supply of water and nutrient solution to the plant through a pump with tubing and an emitter. This is the simplest version there is, and it can easily support a single adult plant.

Step 2: Cut a hole

Take the bucket lid and trace the bottom diameter of the pot on the lid. The bottom of the pot must be slightly smaller than the top of it. You can use a utility knife along with a small drill to cut a hole into the bucket lid. Place the pot in this hole such that it rests snugly within it and the lip of the pot must support the pot in the hole.

Now you will need to drill a hole that's about 1" in diameter into the bucket lid (place it next to the hole you drilled for the plant). You will need to drill another hole near the edge of the container's lid. Place the submersible pump at the bottom of the bucket. Connect this submersible pump with the barbed head of the poly tube. Carefully thread the tubing through the hole drilled near the hole for the plant and run the pump's power cord through the other hole next to it.

Step 3: Nutrient mixture

You will need to add about 2 gallons of nutrient and water mixture to the bucket and screw the lid on to the container.

Step 4: Adjustments

Now you will need to cut the excess tubing such that at least 4-6" of it are left above the lid of the bin or the bucket. Take the spaghetti tube hole punch and punch a hole from the end of the polytube irrigation line—the hole needs to be 1-2" wide. Connect the spaghetti tube to the irrigation tube with a barbed coupling or a clamp. Now, connect the stake and the emitter or dripper onto the other end of the spaghetti tube. Plug the top end of the tube, so the line stays pressurized.

Step 5: Done

The final step is to place the plant in the hole that you drilled in the lid. Place the emitter next to the plant and plug in the power cord to start the supply of solution. You need to change the nutrient solution once every ten days if it is a salt-based solution and once every week if you are using an organic solution.

Evaluate all the different methods of hydroponics that are available and look at their advantages as well as disadvantages. You will need to consider the systems according to whether they are ideal for a specific crop you want to grow or not. For short-term crops like lettuce, you can use systems like ebb and flow, using channels that are made of gravel. While, for long-term crops that are susceptible to root diseases, you must opt for a non-circulating medium-based system. Some of the factors that you must consider are whether the system that you want to opt for will be a good fit for the crops, the environment necessary for their growth, and the water quality, along with the ease of maintenance and their growing period. Apart from this, you will also need to consider the ease with which you can cultivate and harvest the crop, the ability for improving the crop turnaround as well as the installation, replacement, maintenance, and operating costs of the system that you have selected.

The steps given in this section are easy to understand and follow. Also, it doesn't take long to set up a DIY hydroponic garden and you can do it by spending less than 100$.

Chapter Three: Hydroponic Seed Starting

Benefits of Starting with Seeds

A lot of people don't like to start with seeds since it takes more time and effort; however, there are a couple of good reasons why you must do this. It is certainly easier to head to a store and grab some seedlings, place them in the hydroponic system and wait for nature to do its bit, but there are a couple of disadvantages to using store-bought saplings.

The first disadvantage is that you have limited options to choose from. Your options are the only ones that are available at the store. If you decide to grow the plants from seeds, then you can pretty much grow anything that you want to. It gives you free rein over what you want to grow.

If you are starting with seeds, then you don't have to worry about any root damage or the plant going through any trauma of transplantation. Instead, they will naturally get used to their home. Transplantation also opens up the doors for any pest or pathogen infestation.

Apart from this, when you are growing the plants from seeds, it makes the experience more satisfying. Plus, buying seeds is always a cheaper option—instead of shelling out a handful of bucks to purchase seedlings, you can purchase multiple packets of seeds.

Things Needed to Start Seeds

The first time you decide to start from seeds for your home-built hydroponic system, the cost might be slightly higher—think of this as an investment, though. The equipment that you buy will come in handy in the future. Also, you don't need any special equipment for this purpose.

You will need a growing tray with a dome (quite similar to a mini greenhouse) to create the ideal environment for growing the seeds. If you are growing seeds in an area that's slightly cool, then you will also need a heating mat. You will need to place this heating mat under the grow tray to keep the seeds warm. You can also invest in some artificial lights to promote germination. You will need starter cubes like the ones made of Rockwool or stone wool to place the seeds in. It helps in the germination and also makes the seeds comfortable in the hydroponic system.

Steps for Sprouting Seeds

The first thing to do is soak the starter cubes you are using in distilled or clean water for about an hour. After they have been given the opportunity to submerge, place some seeds in the cube's hole. You want to add multiple seeds in case you have seeds that do not germinate. As soon as they germinate, you can start to weed out the weaker plants to allow the strongest ones to grow.

You will need to prep the tray you want to use for growing. To do this, you will need to fill it up with an inch of pure water or mild nutrient solution. Place the light source and the heating mat as necessary. You can screw on the lid to keep the heat and humidity in the tray.

Place these cubes in the growing tray and add pure water or concentrated nutrient solution as the level decreases in the growing tray.

In about four days, you will start to see some sprouts breaking through the surface of the seeds.

Some people prefer to use a Ziploc bag instead of a culture tray when they try to germinate seeds since they function as a greenhouse. Seal the bag with a small amount of air and place it in a dark place for about four days to allow the seeds to germinate. Then you can put seed cubes with the germinated seeds in the culture tray.

Steps for Transplantation

You will need to ensure that the tiny saplings are growing strong with the help of the hydroponic nutrient solution. Once they grow stronger and bigger, you will need to reduce the strength of the nutrient solution by half.

You will be able to start seeing the roots coming out of the bottom of the cube, which is the sign you've been patiently waiting for. Once the roots pop out, it is time for transplantation—this can take up to 2-4 weeks depending on the variety of the plant you are growing.

Clear up some space in the growing medium for the seed, along with its cube. You will need to carefully transplant the starter cube into the growing medium and cover it up gently with some more media.

Allow the roots to naturally seek out water and nutrients by watering the top for a couple of days. This also allows the root system to develop.

And, voila! Your work is done! You managed to grow the seedlings from seeds, and they have transplanted into strong plants. According to the plants that you are growing, you can expect your first harvest in about 4 to 8 weeks after the transplantation.

Chapter Four: Best Plants for Hydroponics

Now that you know about the different types of hydroponics systems, their setup, and the different growing methods, the next step is to select the plants you want to grow. You can pretty much grow anything that you want, but here is a list of the best-suited plants for hydroponics.

Lettuces

The ideal temperature for lettuces needs to be cold, and the desirable pH is between 6 and 7. They are the perfect ingredient for all salads and are the most commonly grown plants with hydroponics. They don't take long to grow and are quite easy to take care of. The ideal hydroponics systems for lettuces are NFT, aeroponics and an ebb and flow system. This is the best plant to start with for a beginner.

Tomatoes

They need a slightly warmer climate to grow, and the desirable pH is between 5.5 and 6.5. Different types of tomatoes, like the regular ones and the cherry varieties, are usually grown by a hydroponic hobbyist as well as commercial growers. Technically, a tomato is a fruit, but many seem to think of them as vegetables. One thing that you must be aware of while growing tomatoes is that they need plenty of light. So, you will need to invest in good growing lights if you plan to grow them indoors.

Radishes

They need a slightly cold climate to grow, and the desirable pH is between 6 and 7. Radishes are full of flavor, and they also make for a good flavoring mix when combined with other vegetables. Radishes are quite easy to grow in the soil as well as with hydroponic systems. Starting them with seeds is ideal—the seeds take less than a week to sprout. They tend to thrive in cold climates, so you don't have to worry about any lighting.

Kale

They need a moderate climate (cool to warm) to grow, and the desirable pH is between 5.5 and 6.5. Not only is kale a superfood, but they are quite tasty as well. You can add them to any dish to drive up its nutrient value. It is quite easy to grow kale, and it is ideal for a beginner. Kale tends to thrive when grown hydroponically and it doesn't need much maintenance.

Cucumbers

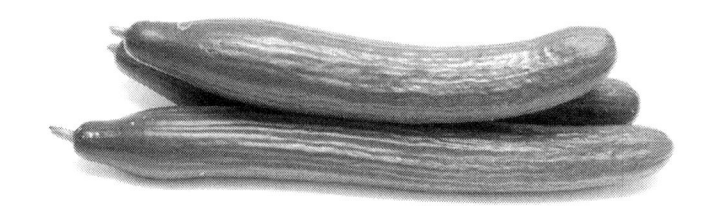

They need a slightly warmer climate to grow, and the desirable pH is between 5.5 and 6. They are common vines and can be grown indoors as well as in commercial greenhouses. Under the right climatic conditions, they proliferate and give out a high yield. There are different types and sizes you can choose from—you can opt for the thick-skinned American cucumbers, the long and thin-skinned European seedless variety or even the smooth-skinned Lebanese cucumber. As long as you provide them with a warm climate and sufficient light, the cucumber vines will thrive.

Spinach

They need a slightly moderate climate to grow (cold to warm), and the desirable pH is between 6 and 7. You can either add it to a salad raw or cook it. Spinach tends to thrive in a water-based growing environment. It is adapted to cold growing conditions, so it doesn't need much light. You can either tear off a couple of leaves as and when you need them or even harvest it all at once. If you can provide the right growing environment, you can get up to 12 weeks of continuous harvest.

Beans

They need a slightly warmer climate to grow, and the desirable pH is 6. Beans are not only low-maintenance but can also prove to be quite productive. There are multiple types of beans to choose from, like green beans, lima beans, pinto beans, and pole beans. You need a vertical stake like a trellis or something else to help the pole beans grow. They take about three to eight days to germinate. You can start harvesting them within six to eight weeks. After that, you will notice a conventional crop for three to four months.

Chives

They need a slightly warm to hot climate to grow, and the desirable pH is 6. It is quite easy to grow chives from a plant instead of seeds. So, it is a good idea to purchase some plants from a local gardening supply store. It takes about six to eight weeks for the chives to fully mature under favorable conditions. Once they are mature, you can start harvesting them once every three to four weeks and wait for them to regrow. Remember that chives need a lot of light—about 12 hours of light every day.

Basil

Basil needs a slightly warmer climate to grow, and the desirable pH is between 5.5 and 6.5. Basil is one of the resilient varieties that thrive in a hydroponic system. It is therefore not a surprise that it's the most widely grown herb in hydroponic gardening. It is best suited for drip and NFT systems of hydroponics. You can start harvesting the leaves on a weekly basis once the plant is mature. Basil requires a lot of light, and any deficiency in it will result in poor growth and yield. Ensure that you expose it to light for at least 10 hours per day.

Mint

Mint needs a slightly warmer climate to grow, and the desirable pH is between 5.5 and 6. Mints such as spearmint and peppermint are extensively grown using hydroponics. They are quite aromatic, flavorful, refreshing, and pungent (in a good way). They can be easily added to food as well as beverages. The roots of these plants spread rather quickly, so using hydroponics to grow them is a good idea.

Strawberries

They need a slightly warmer climate to grow, and the desirable pH is 6. They are quite suited for hydroponics. They are the most commercially produced fruits using hydroponics. The NFT system is the best method to grow strawberries. Once the plant is fully mature, you can enjoy a fresh bounty all year long.

Blueberries

They need a slightly warmer climate to grow, and the desirable pH is between 4.5 and 6. The best method to grow them is using an NFT hydroponics system. Growing them from seeds is difficult, so I suggest you grow them by transplanting. These plants take longer to bear fruits, so you will need to be quite patient with them.

Peppers

They need a slightly warmer climate to grow, and the desirable pH is between 5.5 and 6. They need a growing condition that's quite similar to that of tomatoes. Peppers can take anywhere between two to three months to fully mature. You can either start them from seeds or even from plants. The ideal varieties of peppers to choose from are jalapeno and habanero.

Growing crops in summer is easy, but with the

help of hydroponics, you can grow crops in any season. The main reason for this is that the plants no longer have to expend a major chunk of their energy reserves for seeking nutrients by sending out their routes, and hence they have more energy for growing. Another advantage of hydroponics is that you don't need to tend to your garden every single day. If you have built a hydroponic system that can water automatically, then you can go on a vacation without having to worry about your precious garden. You needn't worry about watering or weeding either. During winter, you can harvest tomatoes, cucumbers, lettuce, and other greens, by making use of your hydroponic system. It is a cheery sight when you can see your vegetables, fruits, and herbs flowering, sitting under the grow light when you have snow billowing outside. In spring, you can move your hydroponic system to a porch or a balcony, or even into the greenhouse so that you can utilize sunlight. You will be able to harvest your ripe tomatoes grown in the hydroponic system at least two months before than those harvested by dirt farmers because the plants have been able to grow even during the winter.

Chapter Five: Hydroponic Nutrients

There are two segments that I will cover in this chapter. The first segment deals with the selection of nutrients, and the second deals with the mixing of these nutrients.

You have two options when it comes to providing nutrients for your plants; you can either purchase a premixed ready-to-use nutrient mixture, or make one at home by yourself. If you are using premixed nutrients, then you can assure yourself that the plants will be getting all the nutrients that they need for their growth. However, this amount will depend on the amount of water you are adding to the ready-to-use mixture. If you are mixing your nutrients at home, then it gives you total control over the nutrients you feed the plant, and it is quite economical. Also, it enables us to ensure that you are using only organic materials.

Selecting the Nutrients

Before you can jump into selecting the nutrients that you want to use, there are a couple of things that you must do.

The first thing that you need to do is understand the composition of the water you will use. To do this, all that you need to do is send a sample of the water to a lab and get it tested. If the water is soft, then you can add the necessary nutrients to it to make it fit for the plants you want to grow. If the water is hard, then you will need to filter it out and get rid of all heavy metals before you can use it. You need to get the water tested from time to time to ensure that it is fit for growing plants, if not you will be merely harming the plants. The common elements present in regular tap water are calcium carbonate and magnesium carbonate, which are desirable in limited quantities. So, if you are aware of their existing levels, you can add or subtract certain nutrients accordingly.

The next thing that you need to do is familiarize yourself with the different nutrients that are essential for a plant's growth, like calcium nitrate, potassium, phosphorus, magnesium sulfate, and monopotassium phosphate; water is formed when hydrogen and oxygen are fused; sulfur and nitrogen provide amino acids and other proteins; phosphorus is essential for photosynthesis; potassium and magnesium are essential for the synthesis of certain starches and sugars; calcium is essential for the growth of cells and the building up of cell walls; and nitrogen and magnesium help generate chlorophyll, which is necessary for photosynthesis.

Now you will need to carefully select the micronutrients necessary for the growth of the plant. Micronutrients are also known as trace elements, and they are needed in small quantities for the growth of the plant. They tend to affect the growth and reproductive abilities of the plant. The trace elements that you need to include are copper, iron, zinc, boron, manganese, chlorine, nickel, cobalt, sodium, molybdenum, and silicon. You can add up to 10 micronutrients to the nutrient mixture.

You will need to check the temperature of the water, also. If the water is too hot or frigid, then the seeds will not germinate. Also, if the water isn't of ideal temperature, then it can severely damage the roots of the plant. The ideal temperate must be between 64°F and 80°F.

Plants suited for cold climates will grow well even if the water is colder, and vice versa with plants for warmer climates in warmer water. Whenever you are adding fresh water to the reservoir, you must ensure that it is of the right temperature.

The final thing you need to consider is the pH of the water you use. The ideal pH level for the growth of a plant is between 5.5 and 7. So, keep a pH meter handy at all times and check the pH of the water at least once every week. If the pH levels keep fluctuating, then it will hurt the plant's health. It also affects the plant's ability to absorb and synthesize nutrients. Before you go ahead and add any nutrients to the water, you need to check its pH.

Nutrient Mixture

The first thing that you must do is take a couple of containers and fill it up with distilled water or water that has gone through reverse osmosis. If you don't have access to distilled water, then use tap water that has been left in the open for 24 hours, to remove traces of any chlorine from it. If you are using tap water, please make sure that you get it tested first.

Now, you will need to measure out all the nutrients you want to use. Use a graduated cylinder or a beaker to measure liquids and a chemical scoop to portion out the fertilizers.

You don't necessarily need a funnel to mix the ingredients but having one will certainly ensure that nothing spills—it is also easier to pour chemicals when you use a small funnel. Some nutrients can cause skin irritation, and so using a funnel helps to prevent this.

Once you add the nutrients to the water, you must check its overall pH to ensure that it is safe for the plants. Even a slight imbalance in the level of nutrients or the pH level can seriously harm your plants and damage their roots. Also, ensure that there is sufficient nutrient solution in the reservoir so that the pump doesn't start pumping air. Before you add the nutrient mixture to the water in the reservoir, please stir it.

NPK (nitrogen, phosphorus, and potassium) is the most common ratio of macros that a plant needs for its growth. The ratio of NPK shows the concentration of these elements. For instance, an NPK ratio of 10:5:8 means that for every ten molecules of nitrogen, there are 5 and 8 molecules of phosphorus and potassium present respectively.

When a plant is developing its roots, then it will need a lot of potassium and phosphorus. While it is growing, then it needs more nitrogen and potassium. During the flowering stage, it needs more phosphorus than the other two nutrients. So, you must keep the stage of plant's development in mind when you are making the nutrient mix. An all-purpose nutrient blend has a 10:10:10 or a 20:20:20 ratio.

Follow the simple tips given in this chapter to ensure that the plants get all the nutrients that they need.

Chapter Six: Lighting Guide

In this section, you will learn about a couple of common lighting examples suited for indoor growing.

HPS (high-pressure sodium) lamps are usually used for flowering plants or during the flowering phase of plants. Their spectrum output is usually between 2,000 and 3,000K (Kelvins—a measure of thermodynamic temperature), and they give off a yellow or orange light.

MH (metal halide) lamps are usually used for the vegetative phase of the plant, and has a spectrum of somewhere in between 4,000 and 6,500K. They give out a blue or a white light.

T5 lamps are fluorescent battens that are

usually used during the germination of seeds or propagation from cuttings. They're great lights to use for seedlings, especially before transitioning them to something with a higher intensity.

CFLs—or compact fluorescent lamps— are quite similar to T5 lights and are also pretty much used for the same reasons. The only difference is that a CFL offers little power and allows the grower to use the same light for about three weeks before transitioning.

LEC stands for light emitting ceramic. It is a rather new introduction, and these lights tend to give out greater micromoles per watt than MH or HPS lights. This means that the spectrum of this light is closer to natural sunlight than any others. You can use these throughout the life of the plant, and the spectrum ranges from 3,000 to 4,500K. They only come in a 315W variation and give out

600W. So, they are sustainable in the long run, and they also increase the production of essential resins by up to 40%.

LED stands for light emitting diode—this technology has been around for a while now. The LEDs are rather an all-in-one kind of light, offering complete spectrum, 3-5 diodes, and are also available in different wattages. Professional growers tend to use them along with HPS lights.

LEP—or light emitting plasma—is a new technology. The power usage of these lights is quite sustainable, and they are a good option for a conscious grower. They offer a unique spectrum that ranges between 10,000 and 14,000K. They come in handy to support flowering plants, especially when used with HPS lights.

Chapter Seven: Maintenance and Troubleshooting

Keep it Clean

The first thing that you need to do is ensure that, even before you set it all up, you keep the setting clean and you clean the plant box with some mild, 10% bleach.

You will need to prune the leaves to prevent the growth of fungus.

You need to remove all the diseased plants as well.

Also, change the water in the reservoir. When you are doing this, clean the reservoir with a

10% bleach solution before you add the nutrient and water mixture to it.

Drippers

If you are using a drip system, always keep a couple of extra drippers handy. This helps when you need to change the clogged drippers. Place the clogged drippers in a solution of water and vinegar to unclog them.

Ebb and Flow System

You need a timer that can be set for 5-minute intervals to ensure that the growing medium is soaked in the nutrient solution for 10 minutes at a time.

Top your plants with water to wash away the excess salts from it and do this once a week.

pH

The pH of the growing medium must always be between 5 and 7. If it goes anywhere outside of this range, the plants cannot absorb the nutrients.

Use a pH meter to check the pH levels frequently—ideally, you need to do this daily but at least once a week.

You will need to change the reservoir solution once a week. Top it off with water and the nutrient mix to adjust its ph.

Calcium Deficiency

If the young leaves start to curl downward, then this is an indicator of calcium deficiency. If old leaves start curling up, then there is a problem with its root areas.

Insufficient movement of water causes calcium deficiency. High humidity also reduces the absorption of calcium.

So, by paying close attention to the plants, you will know what needs to be done to rectify such a deficiency.

Incorrect Lighting

Investing in the wrong lighting can destroy your hydroponic garden. Too little light and the plants cannot photosynthesize their nutrients. If the lighting is too harsh, then it will burn your plants.

Nutrient Deficiency

The right composition and formulation of the nutrient solution are essential for the plant's growth. The most common deficiency that a plant faces is the deficiency of potassium, nitrogen, iron, calcium or magnesium. A high level of potassium causes magnesium deficiency. Iron deficiency is due to a cold growing environment or when the pH levels are too high.

A simple way to fix these is by ensuring that you accurately measure all the nutrients that you add to the nutrient mix. You also need to get an accurate reading of the conductivity, temperature, pH level and other important nutrients of the solution.

Algae Growth

Water, nutrients, and light induce the growth of algae. Algae growth can be green, red, black or even brown, and they are a slimy growth that sticks onto the channels, pumps, and the growing medium. They also give off an earthy or moldy smell and can clog up the dripper, pumps, and the filters.

A small number of algae are tolerable, but when its growth becomes excessive, then it can be quite problematic. To fix this, you need to clear the entire hydroponic system and start afresh.

Also, algae grow in water when the reservoir is

exposed to light, so ensure that the reservoir is opaque and no light can pass through it.

Pests and Pathogens

Most pests and pathogens that plague plants and grow in soil are eliminated when you use hydroponics, but when you opt for indoor hydroponics, there are certain things that you must be wary of.

You need to protect the plants from spider mites, fungus gnats, whiteflies, aphids, and Pythium, along with fungi and mold. To do this, spray the plants with pesticides (organic or chemical).

Reviews are one of the most important factors in a book's success. Even if you are a bestselling author, your new book--which you have toiled on for years--can have its chances of success ruined within a matter of moments by a few negative reviews (genuine or not).

It would mean so much to me if you would take a moment to visit the page (or any of my other titles) on a few of the major retailers and vote on the existing reviews (or place a review yourself). If you don't wish to write a review, you can still help by simply voting Helpful or Unhelpful (or Thumbs up or Down) to the top 10 or so reviews. As always, please feel free to leave an honest review, whether positive or negative. And if you vote or review one of my books (positive or negative, of course!) Please let me know.

To vote or review, just click on the link below.

https://amzn.to/2T9cKEP

Thanks! Now, continue on to the next page

Conclusion

I want to thank you once again for purchasing this book.

Now that you have reached the end of this book, I am certain that you are equipped with all the information that you will possibly need to start your hydroponics garden at home.

Hydroponics is quite simple once you understand how it all works. You no longer need to worry about the quality of soil or the space available to start a garden—gone are the days when you needed space in your front or your back yard to start one.

All that you need to do now is select a method of hydroponics you want to use, gather the necessary supplies, build the hydroponic system, and start growing the plants that you want to. What's more, hydroponics is inexpensive, and you can successfully start hydroponic gardening by spending less than $100.

You will need to be patient with the plants, tend to them, and ensure that no pest or insects trouble them. A little patience, time, effort, and care are all that is needed to start and maintain your garden.

Hydroponics is here to stay, and in fact, these days it is commercially adapted for mass production. Hydroponics is certainly the future of agriculture. So, what are you waiting for? Jump on this bandwagon and ride into the future with hydroponics. This sustainable and economical option is better than soil cultivation. You can now start to grow fresh, organic produce within the comfort of your home. They need little to no maintenance, so it certainly does sound like a win-win.

All the best!

Bonus Materials

Get the complete table that includes the ***Electro-Conductivity (EC) and parts per million (PPM)*** for all the plants below at the ***FREE BONUS Section (+ Free Cheat Sheet)***.

Vegetables	pH	Conductivity Factor (cF)
Lettuce	5.5-6.5	8.0-12
Spinach	5.5-6.6	18-23
Bok Choy	6.5-7.0	15-20
Tomato	5.5-6.5	20-50
Pepper	5.8-6.3	20-30
Cucumber	5.8-6.0	17-25
Celery	6.5	18-24
Bean (Common)	6	20-40
Cauliflower	6.0-7.0	5.0-12
Okra	6.5	20-24
Potato	5.0-6.0	20-25
Radishes	6.0-7.0	16-22

| Cabbage | 6.5-7.0 | 25-30 |

Herbs	pH	Conductivity Factor (cF)
Basil	5.5-6.5	10 to 16
Green Mint	5.5-6.0	20-24
Chives	6.0-6.5	18-22
Rosemary	5.5-6.0	10 to 16
Thyme	5.5-7.0	8.0-16
Lemon balm	5.5-6.5	10 to 16
Parsley	5.5-6.0	8.0-18

Fruits	pH	Conductivity Factor (cF)
Blueberry	4.0-5.0	18-20
Banana	5.5-6.5	18-22
Red Currant	6	14-18
Strawberries	5.5-6.5	18-22

Flowers	pH	Conductivity Factor (cF)
Chrysanthemum	6.0-6.2	18-25
Roses	5.5-6.0	15-25
Palms	6.0-7.5	16-20
Ferns	6	16-20
Aster	6.0-6.5	18-24
Dracena	5.0-6.0	18-24
Dieffenbachia	5	18-24
Carnation	6	20-35

Free Bonus!

A Cheat Sheet of 10 Unrestricted Indoor Gardening Tips for Beginners to Start Growing Immediately (Additional pH & Nutrient Table for Hydroponic Plants)

https://bit.ly/2T18mI6

Simply as a 'Thank You' for purchasing this book, take this **FREE PDF Cheat Sheet and Additional pH & Nutrient Table for**

Hydroponic Plants by accessing on the link above to help you get started off on your hydroponic journey. These are some tips of indoor gardening that will **definitely give you a head start** on building your hydroponic system. It includes tip with dealing indoor plants insects, caring your plants, choosing the right indoor plant and many more. Furthermore, there is a simple instruction on building a DIY Craft for gardening that even you can do it together with your children's.

Made in the USA
Lexington, KY
24 April 2019